Haslings

Comprehension Activities in Poetry: Grade Four

Table of Contents

Unit One: Fun and Wonder

Unit Two: Imagination

Unit Three: Outside My Window

Unit Four: Tales to Tell

Comprehension Activities in Poetry: Grade Four

Introduction

This book is designed to help students become better readers through the reading of poetry. The IRA/NCTE Standards for the English Language Arts list as their first recommendation: "Students read a wide range of print and nonprint texts to build an understanding of texts, of themselves, and of the cultures of the United States and the world...." Poetry is a form of literature easily read and enjoyed by young students. First books often use the rhythm and rhyme of poetry to engage young readers. Because poetry often uses figurative speech, it encourages imagination and creative thinking. As students progress, their enjoyment of poetry grows to encompass different forms and styles. Most students not only enjoy the reading of poetry, but they will also enjoy creating their own verse, both in the school setting and on their own. It is recommended that students encounter a variety of reading selections to hold their interest. Poetry should be included at every grade level.

Because of its language, poetry often lends itself to individual interpretation. However, for the young reader, poetry is more often fun and straightforward. Students' comprehension of the reading of poetry can be tested through questions designed to encourage them to think about their reading. The questions in this book test students' comprehension on six levels: finding the facts, detecting a sequence, learning new vocabulary through context, identifying the main idea, drawing conclusions, and making inferences. Strengthening these skills through the reading of poetry will also aid students in other reading experiences.

Organization

The poems in this book are divided into thematic units to help the teacher to integrate the poetry into other areas of study. The units are Fun and Wonder, Imagination, Outside My Window, and Tales to Tell. All of the units include the six comprehension skills listed earlier. Each poem is followed by six comprehension questions, always in the same order. The questions increase in difficulty from literal understanding of the text to more complex thinking and reasoning skills. The order of the questions and a brief description of the skills follow:

- **Facts:** The first question focuses on literal comprehension. Students identify pieces of factual information. They look for specific details that tell who, what, when, where, and how.

- **Sequence:** The second question refers to sequence. Students practice identifying the order of events or the steps in a process.

- **Context:** The third question requires students to practice using all the words in the poem to understand unfamiliar words. Students become aware of the relationships between words, phrases, and sentences. Mastering the use of context enables students to become independent readers.

- **Main Idea:** The fourth question deals with the main idea of the poem. Students will identify the overall point made in the poem. Students must be able to differentiate between the main idea and the details that support it.

- **Conclusion:** The fifth question requires students to draw conclusions. Conclusions are not stated in the reading but must be formulated by the student. Students must draw conclusions based only on the information in the poem. They must put together the details from the information as if they were clues to a puzzle. The conclusion students draw must be supported by the details in the poem.

- **Inference:** The sixth question asks students to make inferences. Students make inferences by combining their own knowledge and experiences with what they read. They put together the facts in the poem with what they already know to make a reasonable inference about something that is not stated in the poem. Making inferences requires students to go beyond the information in the poem.

Along with the six questions, each poem is followed by an extension activity related to poetry or the specific poem. The extension activities are designed to further the students' appreciation and understanding of reading and writing poetry.

The assessment at the beginning of the book can be used as a pretest to gauge the students' reading comprehension skills. It can also be used as a posttest to determine improvements in reading comprehension skills when the students have completed the exercises.

Use
The activities in this book are designed for independent use by students who have had instruction in the specific skills covered in the lessons. This book should serve as additional practice with reading comprehension skills. Copies of the activity sheets can be given to individuals or pairs of students for completion. The poems and activities can be used as a center activity. When the students are familiar with the content of the worksheets, they can be assigned as homework.

To begin, determine the implementation that fits your students' needs and your classroom structure. The following plan suggests a format for this implementation.

1. Administer the Assessment to establish baseline information on each student. This test may also be used as a posttest when the student has completed the book.

2. Explain the purpose of the worksheets to the class.

3. Review the mechanics of how you want the students to work with the activities. Do you want them to work in pairs? Are the activities for homework?

4. Introduce the students to the process and purpose of the activities. Work with the students when they have difficulty. Give them only one poem at a time to avoid pressure.

5. Read a poem together. Review with the students each comprehension skill by using the poem's activities as a practice example. Read through the extension activity together.

Note: Some of the poems in this book may contain language or references that will challenge some students. All students will benefit from an initial group reading of these poems and the opportunity to discuss them. Provide time for the students to ask questions regarding meaning and language.

Integrating Poetry into the Curriculum
Improving reading comprehension skills in language arts has obvious merits for other areas of study as well. Reading and writing skills are important in all curriculum areas, and language arts are naturally integrated into all subject areas through vocabulary, descriptions, reading directions, and answering questions.

Poetry is a form of literature that can be easily brought into other curriculum areas through subject matter. Poems about nature and animals go hand-in-hand with science studies. Poems concerning people and places complement social studies. Poems about numbers and sequence can bring literature to math class. The rhythm and rhyme of poems have always been a part of music, dance, and games. The descriptive language of poetry lends itself to artwork and imagination. The fun and pleasure of poetry can be used to enrich learning across the curriculum.

Poetry and the 4-Blocks Model

The 4-Blocks Model for teaching is based on the premise that there are four basic approaches to teaching reading. Students are exposed to all four approaches each day. Each block has something different to offer each student, and no student is left out of the learning process. Though the model was designed for younger grades, specifically first and second, adaptations can be applied to make it work at higher levels. The four blocks are guided reading, self-selected reading, working with words, and writing. Although each block must be taught each day, and a pre-subscribed amount of time allotted to each block, teachers may decide when each block best fits into his or her class time. In other words, there is no correct order in which to teach the blocks.

The purpose of the **guided reading** block is to expose students to many different types of print items. The teacher may begin the block by discussing the topic of the reading selection. He or she may provide necessary background information. This block focuses on comprehension skills. Since rereading and understanding are the focus, this format works well for introducing poetry.

The **self-selected reading** block may begin with a teacher reading. Then the students choose books that they want to read. To encourage familiarity with poetry, many different books of verse and poems should be available to choose from.

The **working with words** block helps the students to remember frequently misspelled words and high-frequency words. It includes a "word wall" where the words are easily accessible. The block focuses on spelling strategies and writing skills as opposed to vocabulary and reading skills. High-frequency and frequently misspelled words from the poems would be included on the word wall.

The **writing** block concentrates on all aspects of writing. The teacher discusses the habits of good writers, editing techniques, inventive spelling, illustrating, and beginning and ending stories. The students choose their best writing for publishing and sharing. Poetry could easily be incorporated into the writing block.

The 4-Blocks Model has proved to be a successful tool for teaching reading and writing skills in many schools across the nation. It is naturally more complex than the brief summary given here. More information on the 4-Blocks Model can be found at http://www.teachers.net

Come Out to Play

by Mother Goose

Girls and boys, come out to play,
The moon doth shine as bright as day;
Leave your supper, and leave your sleep,
And come with your playfellows into the street.
Come with a whoop, come with a call,
Come with a good will or not at all.
Up the ladder and down the wall,
A half-penny roll will serve us all.
You find milk, and I'll find flour,
And we'll have a pudding in half an hour.

Go on to the next page.

Come Out to Play, p. 2

DIRECTIONS → Think about the poem. Then answer these questions. Darken the circle by the correct answer.

1. Who is this poem about?

Ⓐ bakers

Ⓑ parents

Ⓒ children

2. Before having pudding, the children will

Ⓐ eat dinner.

Ⓑ find flour and milk.

Ⓒ wait an hour.

3. When the poem says, "Come with a good will," it means

Ⓐ be kind.

Ⓑ bring money.

Ⓒ be willing to make pudding.

4. This poem is mostly about

Ⓐ a dark night.

Ⓑ a lonely child.

Ⓒ things children do.

5. The setting for this poem is

Ⓐ in the afternoon.

Ⓑ in the morning.

Ⓒ at night.

6. You can tell that the person in the poem

Ⓐ likes to argue with his friends.

Ⓑ likes to have fun with other children.

Ⓒ does not sleep at night.

[from] The Elephant's Child

by Rudyard Kipling

I keep six honest serving-men
   (They taught me all I knew);
Their names are What and Why and When
   And How and Where and Who.
I send them over land and sea,
   I send them east and west;
But after they have worked for me,
   I give them all a rest.

I let them rest from nine till five,
   For I am busy then,
As well as breakfast, lunch, and tea,
   For they are hungry men.
But different folk have different views;
   I know a person small—
She keeps ten million serving-men,
   Who get no rest at all!

She sends 'em abroad on her own affairs,
   From the second she opens her eyes—
One million Hows, two million Wheres,
   And seven million Whys!

Go on to the next page.

[from] The Elephant's Child, p. 2

DIRECTIONS Think about the poem. Then answer these questions. Darken the circle by the correct answer.

1. When does the poet let the serving-men rest?

   Ⓐ all night
   Ⓑ in the afternoon
   Ⓒ from nine until five

2. The serving-men rest

   Ⓐ before they go to work for the young person.
   Ⓑ after they have worked for the poet.
   Ⓒ while they are working.

3. The poem says, "different folk have different views." "Views" are

   Ⓐ windows.
   Ⓑ ideas.
   Ⓒ feelings.

4. The main idea of this poem is

   Ⓐ young people never stop asking questions.
   Ⓑ people should give their workers a rest.
   Ⓒ no one should talk during meals.

5. The serving-men are

   Ⓐ real people.
   Ⓑ lazy men.
   Ⓒ questions.

6. You can tell that the small person the poet knows

   Ⓐ is very quiet.
   Ⓑ asks many questions.
   Ⓒ is not curious.

POETRY PATCH This poem talks about the words *who, what, where, when,* and *how*. Write a poem about something you have done. In the poem, tell whom it is about, what happened, and when, where, and how it happened.

The Blind Men and the Elephant *[excerpt]*

by Godfrey Saxe

It was six men of Indostan
To learning much inclined,
Who went to see the elephant
(Though all of them were blind),
That each by observation
Might satisfy his mind.

The *First* approached the Elephant,
And happening to fall
Against his broad and sturdy side,
At once began to bawl:
"God bless me! but the Elephant
Is very like a wall!"

The *Second,* feeling of the tusk,
Cried, "Ho! what have we here,
So very round and smooth and sharp?
To me 'tis mighty clear—
This wonder of an Elephant
Is very like a spear!"

The *Third* approached the animal,
And happening to take
The squirming trunk within his hands,
Thus boldly up and spake:
"I see," quoth he, "the Elephant
Is very like a snake!"

The *Fourth* reached out an eager hand,
And felt about the knee.
"What most this wondrous beast is like
Is mighty plain," quoth he;
"'Tis clear enough the Elephant
Is very like a tree!"

The *Fifth,* who chanced to touch the ear,
Said: "Even the blindest man
Can tell what this resembles most;
Deny the fact who can,
This marvel of an Elephant
Is very like a fan!"

The *Sixth* no sooner had begun
About the beast to grope,
Than, seizing on the swinging tail
That fell within his scope,
"I see," quoth he, "the Elephant
Is very like a rope!"

And so these men of Indostan
Disputed loud and long,
Each in his own opinion
Exceeding stiff and strong,
Though each was partly in the right,
And all were in the wrong!

Go on to the next page.

The Blind Men and the Elephant *[excerpt]*, p. 2

DIRECTIONS ➤ **Think about the poem. Then answer these questions. Darken the circle by the correct answer.**

1. The six men in the poem are

  Ⓐ deaf.

  Ⓑ young.

  Ⓒ blind.

2. The third man who touches the elephant thinks

  Ⓐ that the elephant is like a tree.

  Ⓑ that the elephant is like a snake.

  Ⓒ that the elephant is like a fan.

3. The six men disputed about what they had touched. "Disputed" means

  Ⓐ discussed.

  Ⓑ agreed.

  Ⓒ argued.

4. The main idea of this poem is that

  Ⓐ blind men cannot know what is right.

  Ⓑ a tiny bit of information about something is not enough to make a decision about it.

  Ⓒ it takes only a short time to be an expert about something.

5. You can tell that the six men

  Ⓐ think they are very wise.

  Ⓑ know a lot about elephants.

  Ⓒ do not know each other well.

6. Which word would best describe the six men?

  Ⓐ brilliant

  Ⓑ sloppy

  Ⓒ foolish

POETRY PATCH　Draw a picture of one of the six men and the elephant. Write the verse about what is happening under your picture. Include the title of the poem, the poet's name, and write *from* before the title.

Comical Folk

by Mother Goose

In a cottage in Fife
Lived a man and his wife
Who, believe me, were comical folk;
For, to people's surprise,
They both saw with their eyes,
And their tongues moved whenever they spoke!

When they were asleep,
I'm told, that to keep
Their eyes open they could not contrive;
They both walked on their feet,
And 'twas thought what they eat
Helped, with drinking, to keep them alive!

Go on to the next page.

Comical Folk, p. 2

 **DIRECTIONS** **Think about the poem. Then answer these questions. Darken the circle by the correct answer.**

1. What helps keep the man and woman alive?

  Ⓐ sleeping with their eyes closed

  Ⓑ eating and drinking

  Ⓒ living in a cottage

2. Which line appears first in the poem?

  Ⓐ "They both walked on their feet."

  Ⓑ "They both saw with their eyes."

  Ⓒ "And their tongues moved whenever they spoke."

3. "Comical" probably means

  Ⓐ rich.

  Ⓑ unhappy.

  Ⓒ funny.

4. This poem is mostly about

  Ⓐ two normal people.

  Ⓑ two very odd people.

  Ⓒ a strange town.

5. You can tell that

  Ⓐ the poet does not eat or drink.

  Ⓑ the poet is writing for fun.

  Ⓒ the poet is afraid of the people.

6. Which of these is probably true about the people in the poem?

  Ⓐ They probably sleep upside down.

  Ⓑ They probably wear their clothes backwards.

  Ⓒ They probably eat just like everyone else.

POETRY PATCH   This poem uses rhyming words. This is one way that poems can sound different from other kinds of writing. Circle the rhyming words in the poem, and write each rhyming pair. Add two more rhyming words of your own to each pair.

Name _____ Date _____

[from] How the Whale Got His Throat

by Rudyard Kipling

When the cabin port-holes are dark and green
    Because of the seas outside
When the ship goes wop (with a wiggle between)
And steward falls into the soup-tureen,
    And trunks begin to slide;
When Nursey lies on the floor in a heap,
And Mummy tells you to let her sleep,
    And you aren't waked or washed or dressed,
Why, then you will know (if you haven't guessed)
You're "Fifty North and Forty West!"

Go on to the next page.

[from] How the Whale Got His Throat, p. 2

DIRECTIONS ▶ Think about the poem. Then answer these questions. Darken the circle by the correct answer.

1. Who falls into the soup?

ⓐ the nurse
ⓑ mommy
ⓒ the steward

2. What happens last in the poem?

ⓐ The ship goes wop.
ⓑ Trunks slide.
ⓒ The poet is not washed.

3. A "tureen" is most likely a

ⓐ basket.
ⓑ bowl.
ⓒ bag

4. A title for this poem could be

ⓐ "The Sleepy Nurse."
ⓑ "Bad Soup."
ⓒ "A Rough Ride."

5. The people in the poem are probably

ⓐ on a ship.
ⓑ in a car.
ⓒ flying in an airplane.

6. "Fifty North and Forty West" describes a spot on the ocean. It is probably

ⓐ a quiet place to sail.
ⓑ a place where the sea is often rough.
ⓒ a place that makes people tired.

POETRY PATCH   This poem comes from a story by Rudyard Kipling called "How the Whale Got His Throat." Kipling wrote a collection of stories called "Just-So Stories." At the end of each story is a poem. Find a book of Kipling's stories in the library, or look on the Internet. Read "How the Whale Got His Throat" or another one of the stories, and write your own poem to go with it. Some of Kipling's words can be tricky, and some are nonsense. Have an adult help you with words you do not understand.

Name _____ Date _____

The Old Woman and the Peddler

by Mother Goose

There was an old woman, as I've heard tell,
She went to market her eggs for to sell;
She went to market all on a market-day,
And she fell asleep on the King's highway.

There came by a peddler whose name was Stout,
He cut her petticoats all round about;
He cut her petticoats up to the knees,
Which made the old woman to shiver and freeze.

When the little old woman first did wake,
She began to shiver and she began to shake;
She began to wonder and she began to cry,
"Lauk a mercy on me, this can't be I!

"But if I be I, as I hope it be,
I've a little dog at home, and he'll know me;
If it be I, he'll wag his little tail,
And if it be not I, he'll loudly bark and wail."

Home went the little woman all in the dark;
Up got the little dog, and he began to bark;
He began to bark, so she began to cry,
"Lauk a mercy on me, this is none of I!"

Go on to the next page.

The Old Woman and the Peddler, p. 2

DIRECTIONS → Think about the poem. Then answer these questions. Darken the circle by the correct answer.

1. What did the peddler do to the woman?

   Ⓐ He stole her eggs.
   Ⓑ He cut her clothes.
   Ⓒ He broke her eggs.

2. The dog began to bark

   Ⓐ before the woman got home.
   Ⓑ when he saw the peddler.
   Ⓒ after he saw the woman.

3. What is a peddler?

   Ⓐ a small dog
   Ⓑ a person who sells things
   Ⓒ a thief

4. This poem is mostly about

   Ⓐ a little dog that will not stop barking.
   Ⓑ a man who steals from an old woman.
   Ⓒ a woman who is confused because her clothing is cut short.

5. You can tell that the woman

   Ⓐ is rather foolish.
   Ⓑ is thinking clearly.
   Ⓒ knows what happened to her clothes.

6. The peddler will most likely

   Ⓐ sell the woman's petticoats.
   Ⓑ wear the woman's petticoats.
   Ⓒ throw away the woman's petticoats.

POETRY PATCH   Divide into groups of four students each. Choose one student in your group to be the narrator, one to be the old woman, one to be the peddler, and one to be the dog. Act out the poem while the narrator says the words. When it is the old woman's turn to speak, the narrator should turn to her so that she can say her lines. Act out your play for the rest of the class.

The Lamplighter

by Robert Louis Stevenson

My tea is nearly ready and the sun has left the sky.
It's time to take the window to see Leerie going by;
For every night at teatime and before you take your seat,
With lantern and with ladder he comes posting up the street.

Now Tom would be a driver and Maria go to sea,
And my papa's a banker and as rich as he can be;
But I, when I am stronger and can choose what I'm to do,
O Leerie, I'll go 'round at night and light the lamps with you!

For we are very lucky, with a lamp before the door,
And Leerie stops to light it as he lights so many more;
And oh! before you hurry by with ladder and with light;
O Leerie, see a little child and nod to him to-night!

Go on to the next page.

The Lamplighter, p. 2

DIRECTIONS → Think about the poem. Then answer these questions. Darken the circle by the correct answer.

1. Why does the poet feel lucky?

   Ⓐ He gets to light the lamps.
   Ⓑ His father is a banker.
   Ⓒ His house has a lamp by the door.

2. What does the child want Leerie to do before he leaves?

   Ⓐ nod to the child in the window
   Ⓑ light the lamp
   Ⓒ come into the house

3. Leerie's lantern is probably used

   Ⓐ to help him see.
   Ⓑ to light the other lamps.
   Ⓒ for both A and B.

4. The main idea of this poem is that

   Ⓐ the child wishes that he could live with Leerie.
   Ⓑ the child thinks that lighting the lamps would be a fun job.
   Ⓒ the child wants to grow up to be like his father.

5. Leerie lights the lamps

   Ⓐ when he is called.
   Ⓑ on stormy afternoons.
   Ⓒ each evening.

6. This poem tells about a time

   Ⓐ before there were electric lights.
   Ⓑ a few years ago.
   Ⓒ in the future.

POETRY PATCH   The child in this poem would like to have Leerie's job. What job would you like to have someday? Write a poem describing a job that you would like to have when you are older and telling why you think you would like it.

Mr. Nobody [excerpt]

anonymous

I know a funny little man,
As quiet as a mouse,
Who does the mischief that is done
In everybody's house!

There's no one ever sees his face,
And yet we all agree
That every plate we break was cracked
By Mr. Nobody.

'Tis he who always tears our books,
Who leaves the door ajar,
He pulls the buttons from our shirts,
And scatters pins afar;
That squeaking door will always squeak
For, prithee, don't you see,
We leave the oiling to be done
By Mr. Nobody.

The finger marks upon the door
By none of us are made;
We never leave the blinds unclosed,
To let the curtains fade;
The ink we never spill; the boots
That lying 'round you see
Are not our boots;
They all belong to Mr. Nobody!

Go on to the next page.

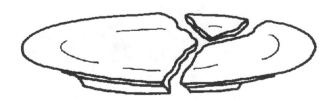

Mr. Nobody *[excerpt]*, p. 2

DIRECTIONS → **Think about the poem. Then answer these questions. Darken the circle by the correct answer.**

1. Who has seen Mr. Nobody?

   Ⓐ only children
   Ⓑ no one
   Ⓒ people who are very quiet

2. Mr. Nobody is blamed

   Ⓐ after something happens.
   Ⓑ before something happens.
   Ⓒ while something is happening.

3. The door is left ajar in the poem. "Ajar" probably means

   Ⓐ alone.
   Ⓑ open.
   Ⓒ broken.

4. Another title for this poem could be

   Ⓐ "The Broken Plate."
   Ⓑ "The Squeaking Door."
   Ⓒ "It Wasn't Me!"

5. The people in the poem blame Mr. Nobody because

   Ⓐ he causes a lot of trouble.
   Ⓑ he is not careful.
   Ⓒ they do not want to get into trouble.

6. The next time something goes wrong,

   Ⓐ the person who is responsible will admit that he or she did it.
   Ⓑ Mr. Nobody will probably be blamed again.
   Ⓒ Mr. Nobody will be asked to find another place to live.

POETRY PATCH Do you have a Mr. Nobody at your house? Write another verse for this poem about things that happen at your house that might be blamed on a Mr. Nobody.

Name _____   Date _____

My Shadow

Robert Louis Stevenson

I have a little shadow that goes in and out with me,
And what can be the use of him is more than I can see.
He is very, very like me from the heels up to the head;
And I see him jump before me, when I jump into my bed.

The funniest thing about him is the way he likes to grow—
Not at all like proper children, which is always very slow;
For he sometimes shoots up taller like an india-rubber ball,
And he sometimes goes so little that there's none of him at all.

He hasn't got a notion of how children ought to play,
And can only make a fool of me in every sort of way.
He stays so close behind me, he's a coward you can see;
I'd think shame to stick to nursie as that shadow sticks to me!

One morning, very early, before the sun was up,
I rose and found the shining dew on every buttercup;
But my lazy little shadow, like an arrant sleepy-head,
Had stayed at home behind me and was fast asleep in bed.

Go on to the next page.

My Shadow, p. 2

DIRECTIONS → **Think about the poem. Then answer these questions. Darken the circle by the correct answer.**

1. The shadow is just like

Ⓐ other children.
Ⓑ the child in the poem.
Ⓒ the child's nurse.

2. When does the shadow go before the child?

Ⓐ when the child goes out to play
Ⓑ when the child sees other children
Ⓒ when the child goes to bed

3. The shadow "hasn't got a notion of how children ought to play." A "notion" is

Ⓐ a thought.
Ⓑ a game.
Ⓒ a question.

4. This poem is mostly about

Ⓐ a child and his nurse.
Ⓑ a child and his shadow.
Ⓒ a child and his friends.

5. The shadow was not with the child at the end of the poem because

Ⓐ the sun was not up yet.
Ⓑ the boy made it stay in bed.
Ⓒ the shadow was tired.

6. The poet most likely wrote this poem

Ⓐ to describe how shadows are formed.
Ⓑ to explain why he has a shadow.
Ⓒ to entertain people.

POETRY PATCH This poem uses comparison and contrast to describe the shadow. Underline parts in the poem where the shadow is compared to something else. This means it is like something else. Circle parts where the shadow is in contrast to something else. This means it is different from something else.

Name _____   Date _____

Adventure

by Hilda Conkling

I went slowly through the wood of shadows,
Thinking always I should meet someone:
There was no one.

I found a hollow
Sweet to rest in all night long:
I did not stay.

I came out beyond the trees
To the moaning sea.
Over the sea swam a cloud the outline of a ship:
What if that ship held my adventure
Under its sails?

Come quickly to me, come quickly,
I am waiting.
I am here on the sand;
Sail close!
I want to go over the waves . . .
The sand holds me back.
Oh adventure, if you belong to me,
Don't blow away down the sky!

Go on to the next page.

Adventure, p. 2

DIRECTIONS → Think about the poem. Then answer these questions. Darken the circle by the correct answer.

1. Where does the poet look for adventure?

   Ⓐ in the city
   Ⓑ in the woods
   Ⓒ in a cave

2. The poet sees the cloud

   Ⓐ after she comes out of the woods.
   Ⓑ after she sleeps in a hollow.
   Ⓒ after she walks on the sand.

3. In this poem, "outline" means

   Ⓐ weight.
   Ⓑ shape.
   Ⓒ size.

4. This poem is mostly about

   Ⓐ a girl taking a walk.
   Ⓑ a girl playing at the beach.
   Ⓒ a girl looking for adventure.

5. The girl does not stay in the woods because

   Ⓐ she does not find what she is looking for.
   Ⓑ the woods are frightening.
   Ⓒ she is looking for the beach.

6. What can you tell about the girl in the poem?

   Ⓐ She does not have any friends.
   Ⓑ She is tired of the things she usually does.
   Ⓒ She has sailed in many ships.

POETRY PATCH   This poem does not use rhyming words. The poet simply wrote her thoughts to tell how she felt and what she saw one day. Write a poem of your own that tells about what you are seeing or feeling. Don't be concerned about rhyming, but just write your thoughts as they come to you.

Rain

by Ebeneezer Jones

More than the wind, more than the snow,
More than the sunshine, I love rain;
Whether it drops soft and low,
Whether it rushes amain.

Dark as the night it spreads its wings,
Slow and silently up on the hills;
Then sweeps over the vale, like a steed that springs
From the grasp of a thousand wills.

Swift sweeps under heaven the raven cloud's flight
And the land and the lakes and the main
Lie belted beneath with steel-bright light,
The light of the swift-rushing rain.

On evenings of summer, when sunlight is low,
Soft the rain falls from opal-hued skies;
And the flowers the most delicate summer can show
Are not stirred by its gentle surprise.

It falls on the pools, and no wrinkling it makes,
But touching melts in, like the smile
That sinks in the face of a dreamer, but breaks
Not the calm of his dream's happy wile.

The grass rises up as it falls on the meads,
The bird softly sings in his bower.
And the circles of gnats circle on like winged seeds
Through the soft sunny lines of the shower.

Go on to the next page.

Name _____ Date _____

Rain, p. 2

 **DIRECTIONS** → **Think about the poem. Then answer these questions. Darken the circle by the correct answer.**

1. What kind of rain does the poet like?

- Ⓐ all kinds
- Ⓑ soft rain
- Ⓒ pouring rain

2. After the soft rain falls on the pools,

- Ⓐ the pools stay smooth.
- Ⓑ the pools overflow with water.
- Ⓒ the water splashes.

3. "Opal-hued skies" are most likely

- Ⓐ sunny.
- Ⓑ clear.
- Ⓒ gray and white.

4. This poem is mostly about

- Ⓐ what troubles the rain has caused for the poet.
- Ⓑ how different kinds of rain look.
- Ⓒ why the poet likes rain the best.

5. The poem says, "circles of gnats circle on." The gnats, or small flies, keep flying because

- Ⓐ the rain is falling down hard.
- Ⓑ the soft rain does not disturb them.
- Ⓒ they like to fly in the rain.

6. If the poet planned to take a walk and it began to rain,

- Ⓐ he would probably change his plans.
- Ⓑ he would probably take a very short walk.
- Ⓒ he would probably enjoy his walk.

POETRY PATCH What kind of weather do you like? Choose windy, sunny, rainy, or snowy, and write an acrostic poem about it. Write the word you choose down the left-hand side of your paper. Then begin each sentence of your poem with the letter at the beginning of each line. For example, if you choose *windy*, the first line of your poem will begin with *w*, the second line will begin with *i*, and so on. Your poem should tell about the weather you choose.

Looking-Glass River

by Robert Louis Stevenson

Smooth it glides upon its travel,
   Here a wimple, there a gleam—
     O the clean gravel!
     O the smooth stream!

Sailing blossoms, silver fishes,
   Pave pools as clear as air—
     How a child wishes
     To live down there!

We can see our colored faces
   Floating on the shaken pool
     Down in cool places,
     Dim and very cool;

'Till a wind or water wrinkle,
   Dipping marten, plumping trout,
     Spreads in a twinkle
     And blots all out.

See the rings pursue each other;
   All below grows black as night,
     Just as if mother
     Had blown out the light!

Patience, children, just a minute—
   See the spreading circles die;
     The stream and all in it
     Will clear by-and-by.

Go on to the next page.

Looking-Glass River, p. 2

DIRECTIONS → **Think about the poem. Then answer these questions. Darken the circle by the correct answer.**

1. What makes the water look dark?

  Ⓐ Something causes ripples in the stream.

  Ⓑ The sunshine is blocked by a cloud.

  Ⓒ Something dark is spilled into the stream.

2. Before the water is disturbed,

  Ⓐ the children go swimming.

  Ⓑ the children can see their faces.

  Ⓒ fish live in the stream.

3. The rings of water "pursue each other." "Pursue" probably means

  Ⓐ soak.

  Ⓑ hurt.

  Ⓒ chase.

4. This poem is mostly about

  Ⓐ how children see a stream.

  Ⓑ how fish live in a stream.

  Ⓒ keeping streams clean.

5. When the surface of the water is still,

  Ⓐ the children will throw rocks into it.

  Ⓑ the fish will hide under rocks.

  Ⓒ the children will see their faces again.

6. You can tell that the children

  Ⓐ have never seen a stream.

  Ⓑ are with an adult.

  Ⓒ will live in the stream.

POETRY PATCH   Meter is the rhythm of a poem. You can count the meter of a poem by counting the syllables in its lines. In some poems, the meter is a very regular pattern, and in others, the pattern is difficult to find. Count the syllables in "Looking-Glass River," and write the number next to each line. Do you see a pattern? Is it a regular pattern?

Name _____   Date _____

Snow in the Suburbs

by Thomas Hardy

Every branch big with it,
Bent every twig with it;
Every fork like a white web-foot;
Every street and pavement mute:
Some flakes have lost their way, and grope back upward, when
Meeting those meandering down they turn and descend again.
The palings are glued together like a wall,
And there is no waft of wind with the fleecy fall.
A sparrow enters the tree,
Whereon immediately
A snow-lump thrice his own slight size
Descends on him and showers head and eyes,
And overturns him,
And near inurns him,
And lights on a nether twig, when its brush
Starts off a volley of other lodging lumps with a rush.
The steps are a blanched slope,
Up which, with feeble hope,
A black cat comes, wide-eyed and thin;
And we take him in.

Go on to the next page.

Snow in the Suburbs, p. 2

DIRECTIONS ➤ **Think about the poem. Then answer these questions. Darken the circle by the correct answer.**

1. The poet takes in

 Ⓐ a sparrow.
 Ⓑ a cat.
 Ⓒ a traveler.

2. After the bird lands in the tree,

 Ⓐ it flies away again.
 Ⓑ the cat frightens it.
 Ⓒ snow almost buries it.

3. The black cat comes up the steps "with feeble hope." "Feeble" probably means

 Ⓐ weak.
 Ⓑ mistaken.
 Ⓒ old.

4. This poem is mostly about

 Ⓐ animals in the cold.
 Ⓑ a snowstorm.
 Ⓒ a bird in a tree.

5. You can tell that

 Ⓐ the poet's family does not care for cats.
 Ⓑ the poet thought the bird was funny.
 Ⓒ the poet's family felt sorry for the cat.

6. It is likely that the poet

 Ⓐ has never seen snow.
 Ⓑ has many other cats.
 Ⓒ has a kind heart for animals.

POETRY PATCH A metaphor is a comparison of two things that are not usually considered alike. This type of comparing does *not* use the words *like* or *as*. For example, "My mother is an angel." This does not say the mother is *like* an angel, but that she *is* an angel. Find the metaphor in "Snow in the Suburbs." (Hint: It is near the end.) Look through other poetry books to find another example of a metaphor.

Name _____ Date _____

Hummingbird

by Hilda Conkling

Why do you stand on the air
And no sun shining?
How can you hold yourself so still
On raindrops sliding?
They change and fall, they are not steady,
But you do not know they are gone.
Is there a silver wire
I cannot see?
Is the wind your perch?
Raindrops slide down your little shoulders...
They do not wet you:
I think you are not real
In your green feathers!
You are not a hummingbird at all
Standing on air above the garden!
I dreamed you the way I dream fairies,
Or the flower I saw yesterday!

Go on to the next page.

Hummingbird, p. 2

 **DIRECTIONS** **Think about the poem. Then answer these questions. Darken the circle by the correct answer.**

1. Where is the hummingbird?

   Ⓐ near the garden
   Ⓑ in the woods
   Ⓒ in the house

2. What does the hummingbird do when the poet sees it?

   Ⓐ flies away
   Ⓑ stands still
   Ⓒ sits on a flower

3. "Steady" means

   Ⓐ not moving.
   Ⓑ not strong.
   Ⓒ not wet.

4. Another title for this poem could be

   Ⓐ "My Garden."
   Ⓑ "An Interesting Little Bird."
   Ⓒ "My Pet Bird."

5. Which word best describes the day?

   Ⓐ sunny
   Ⓑ windy
   Ⓒ rainy

6. Why does the poet mention a silver wire?

   Ⓐ She sees one near the bird.
   Ⓑ She thinks the bird must be held up by one.
   Ⓒ She put the wires in the garden herself.

POETRY PATCH From this poem about a hummingbird, you can tell that a hummingbird is green, small, and can appear to hang in midair. Think of an animal that interests you. Look up some facts, and write a poem about the animal that describes the way it looks and how it behaves. Draw a picture to go with your poem.

Winter Time

by Robert Louis Stevenson

Late lies the wintry sun a-bed,
A frosty, fiery sleepy-head;
Blinks but an hour or two; and then,
A blood-red orange, sets again.

Before the stars have left the skies,
At morning in the dark I rise;
And shivering in my nakedness,
By the cold candle, bathe and dress.

Close by the jolly fire I sit
To warm my frozen bones a bit;
Or with a reindeer-sled, explore
The colder countries 'round the door.

When to go out, my nurse doth wrap
Me in my comforter and cap;
The cold wind burns my face, and blows
Its frosty pepper up my nose.

Black are my steps on silver sod;
Thick blows my frosty breath abroad;
And tree and house, and hill and lake,
Are frosted like a wedding cake.

Go on to the next page.

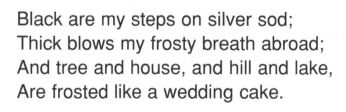

Name _____ Date _____

Winter Time, p. 2

DIRECTIONS Think about the poem. Then answer these questions. Darken the circle by the correct answer.

1. The snowy world makes the poet think of

   Ⓐ ice cream.
   Ⓑ other countries.
   Ⓒ a wedding cake.

2. The child in the poem gets up

   Ⓐ before the sun rises.
   Ⓑ after the house is warm.
   Ⓒ after it is light outside.

3. The poem says, "Black are my steps on silver sod." The child is probably walking on

   Ⓐ the cold floor.
   Ⓑ the snowy ground.
   Ⓒ a silver blanket.

4. This poem is mostly about

   Ⓐ nighttime.
   Ⓑ a child and his nurse.
   Ⓒ winter days.

5. You can tell that

   Ⓐ it is always winter where the child lives.
   Ⓑ the child does not like to be cold.
   Ⓒ the child must stay indoors when it snows.

6. This poem was probably written about

   Ⓐ the future.
   Ⓑ a time many years ago.
   Ⓒ a boy today.

POETRY PATCH   When two things are compared using the words *like* or *as*, it is called a simile. For example, "Her hair was like a mop on her head." Find and circle the simile in this poem. Then write two similes of your own.

The Windmill

by Henry Wadsworth Longfellow

Behold! a giant am I!
   Aloft here in my tower,
   With my granite jaws I devour
The maize, and the wheat, and the rye,
   And grind them into flour.

I look down over the farms;
   In the fields of grain I see
   The harvest that is to be,
And I fling to the air my arms,
   For I know it is all for me.

I hear the sound of flails
   Far off, from the threshing-floors
   In barns, with their open doors,
And the wind, the wind in my sails,
   Louder and louder roars.

I stand here in my place,
   With my foot on the rock below,
   And whichever way it may blow
I meet it face to face,
   As a brave man meets his foe.

And while we wrestle and strive
   My master, the miller, stands
   And feeds me with his hands;
For he knows who makes him thrive,
   Who makes him lord of lands.

On Sundays I take my rest;
   Church-going bells begin
   Their low, melodious din;
I cross my arms on my breast,
   And all is peace within.

Go on to the next page.

The Windmill, p. 2

 **DIRECTIONS** **Think about the poem. Then answer these questions. Darken the circle by the correct answer.**

1. On which day does the windmill stop working?

  Ⓐ Monday

  Ⓑ Wednesday

  Ⓒ Sunday

2. After its "granite jaws" devour the grains,

  Ⓐ the windmill rests.

  Ⓑ the windmill grinds them into flour.

  Ⓒ the miller feeds the windmill.

3. "Devour" has the same meaning as

  Ⓐ destroy.

  Ⓑ eat.

  Ⓒ enjoy.

4. This poem is mostly about

  Ⓐ a man who runs a windmill.

  Ⓑ a town and its windmill.

  Ⓒ what a windmill does.

5. The windmill is clearly

  Ⓐ the only one of its kind.

  Ⓑ very large.

  Ⓒ unhappy with its job.

6. The miller most likely

  Ⓐ relies on the windmill.

  Ⓑ talks to the windmill.

  Ⓒ does not think about the windmill.

POETRY PATCH   Personification is giving objects the feelings and actions of people. In "The Windmill," the windmill seems like a person. It has feelings and it thinks. It speaks of its "arms." Circle the phrases in the poem that make the windmill seem like a human.

The Spider and the Fly *[excerpt]*

by Mary Howitt

"Will you walk into my parlor?" said the spider to the fly;
"'Tis the prettiest parlor that ever you did spy.
The way into my parlor is up a winding stair,
And I have many pretty things to show when you are there."

"O, no, no," said the little fly, "to ask me is in vain,
For who goes up your winding stair can never come down again."

Said the cunning spider to the fly, "Dear friend, what shall I do
To prove the warm affection I've always felt for you?
I have within my pantry good store of all that's nice;
I'm sure you're very welcome. Will you please to take a slice?"

"O, no, no," said the little fly, "kind sir, that cannot be;
I've heard what's in your pantry, and I do not wish to see."

The spider turned him 'round about and went into his den,
For well he knew the silly fly would soon be back again:
So he wove a subtle web in a little corner sly,
And set his table ready to dine upon the fly.
Then he came out to his door again, and merrily did sing,
"Come hither, hither, pretty fly, with the pearl and silver wing:
Your robes are green and purple: there's a crest upon your head;
Your eyes are like the diamond bright, but mine are dull as lead."

Alas, alas! How very soon this silly little fly,
Hearing his wily flattering words, came slowly flitting by.
Up jumped the cunning spider, and fiercely held her fast.
He dragged her up his winding stair, into his dismal den,
Within his little parlor; but she never came out again!

Go on to the next page.

The Spider and the Fly *[excerpt]*, p. 2

 **DIRECTIONS** **Think about the poem. Then answer these questions. Darken the circle by the correct answer.**

1. The way to the spider's parlor is

    Ⓐ down a long hallway.

    Ⓑ through a maze of rooms.

    Ⓒ up a winding stair.

2. The spider set his table

    Ⓐ before he spoke to the fly.

    Ⓑ after he spoke with the fly.

    Ⓒ while the fly was waiting to eat.

3. The spider is cunning. "Cunning" means

    Ⓐ cute.

    Ⓑ sly.

    Ⓒ curious.

4. The main idea of this poem is

    Ⓐ that spiders always get the flies that they go after.

    Ⓑ that spiders have attractive houses that flies can't resist.

    Ⓒ that one should not let flattery convince him or her to make a bad choice.

5. What most likely happens next in the poem?

    Ⓐ The spider eats the fly.

    Ⓑ The spider and the fly have dinner together.

    Ⓒ The spider lets the fly go.

6. The next time the spider wants to get a fly, he will probably

    Ⓐ find a new way to do it.

    Ⓑ not be successful.

    Ⓒ use flattery again.

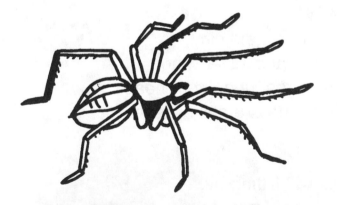

POETRY PATCH   Adjectives are words that describe other words to make writing more interesting. Poets use adjectives to help readers picture what the poet is thinking about. Find the adjectives in "The Spider and the Fly." Circle them. Read the poem aloud. Then try to read the poem aloud without the adjectives. Can you hear the difference?

The Tower and the Falcon

by Hilda Conkling

There was a tower, once,
In a London street.
It was the highest, widest, thickest tower,
The proudest, roundest, finest tower
Of all towers.
English men passed it by:
They could not see it all
Because it went above tree-tops and clouds.

It was lonely up there where the trees stopped
Until one day
A blue falcon came flying.
He cried:
"Tower! Do you know you are the highest, finest, roundest,
The tallest, proudest, greatest,
Of all the towers
In all the world?"

He went away.
That night the tower made a new song
About himself.

Go on to the next page.

The Tower and the Falcon, p. 2

DIRECTIONS Think about the poem. Then answer these questions. Darken the circle by the correct answer.

1. Who spoke to the tower?

- Ⓐ English men
- Ⓑ a sparrow
- Ⓒ a falcon

2. Before the bird came by,

- Ⓐ the tower felt lonely.
- Ⓑ the tower felt grand.
- Ⓒ the tower was tired.

3. The "English men" in the poem probably live in

- Ⓐ Spain.
- Ⓑ France.
- Ⓒ England.

4. This poem is mostly about

- Ⓐ a foreign city.
- Ⓑ a tower.
- Ⓒ a blue falcon.

5. The people who pass by the tower probably

- Ⓐ do not know that it is there.
- Ⓑ do not think much of it because they are used to it.
- Ⓒ speak to it each time they pass.

6. The "new song" that the tower made was most likely

- Ⓐ a happier song.
- Ⓑ a bird's song.
- Ⓒ a lonely song.

POETRY PATCH By now you know that there are many different types of poetry. You probably enjoy some poems more than others. Look through at least three poetry books, and find a poem that you especially enjoy. Share it with your class. If you can, memorize the poem, and recite it to your class instead of reading it aloud. Once you memorize a poem, it will be yours to recite anytime you like. Be sure to say the poet's name and the title of the poem before you recite it.

Wynken, Blynken, and Nod [excerpt]

by Eugene Field

Wynken, Blynken, and Nod one night
    Sailed off in a wooden shoe—
Sailed on a river of crystal light,
    Into a sea of dew.
"Where are you going, and what do you wish?"
    The old moon asked the three.
"We have come to fish for the herring fish

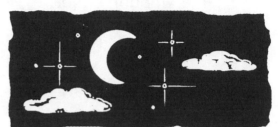

    That live in this beautiful sea;
    Nets of silver and gold have we!"
    Said Wynken, Blynken, and Nod.
All night long their nets they threw
    To the stars in the twinkling foam—
Then down from the skies came the wooden shoe,
    Bringing the fishermen home;
'Twas all so pretty a sail it seemed
    As if it could not be,
And some folks thought 'twas a dream they'd dreamed
    Of sailing that beautiful sea—
    But I shall name you the fishermen three:
        Wynken, Blynken, and Nod.
Wynken and Blynken are two little eyes,
    And Nod is a little head,
And the wooden shoe that sailed the skies
    Is a wee one's trundle-bed.
So shut your eyes while mother sings
    Of wonderful sights that be,
And you shall see the beautiful things
    As you rock in the misty sea,
    Where the old shoe rocked the fishermen three:
        Wynken, Blynken, and Nod.

Go on to the next page.

Wynken, Blynken, and Nod *[excerpt]*, p. 2

DIRECTIONS ▶ **Think about the poem. Then answer these questions. Darken the circle by the correct answer.**

1. Wynken, Blynken, and Nod sailed

   Ⓐ in a boat.
   Ⓑ on the moon.
   Ⓒ in a wooden shoe.

2. After fishing all night,

   Ⓐ the fishermen spoke to the moon.
   Ⓑ they threw their nets to the stars.
   Ⓒ they came down from the stars.

3. The fishermen sailed off "into a sea of dew." "Dew" is

   Ⓐ salt water.
   Ⓑ tiny drops of water.
   Ⓒ a light rain.

4. Another title for this poem could be

   Ⓐ "Fishing for Stars."
   Ⓑ "Fishing with the Moon."
   Ⓒ "The Little Lost Shoe."

5. Wynken, Blynken, and Nod are actually

   Ⓐ great fishermen.
   Ⓑ made-up characters.
   Ⓒ the stars and the moon.

6. This poem was probably written

   Ⓐ to tell about a bad dream.
   Ⓑ as a lullaby for little children.
   Ⓒ as a lesson for fishermen.

POETRY PATCH   "Wynken, Blynken, and Nod" is so full of descriptions that it is easy to imagine what the poet was thinking when he wrote it. What did you picture as you read or heard the poem? Use watercolors to paint a picture that shows what you imagined. Read the poem again for ideas. Include the title of the poem and the poet's name with your painting.

To Any Reader

by Robert Louis Stevenson

As from the house your mother sees
You playing round the garden trees,
So you may see, if you will look
Through the windows of this book,
Another child, far, far away,
And in another garden, play.
But do not think you can at all,
By knocking on the window, call
That child to hear you. He intent
Is all on his play-business bent.
He does not hear, he will not look,
Nor yet be lured out of this book.
For, long ago, the truth to say,
He has grown up and gone away,
And it is but a child of air
That lingers in the garden there.

Go on to the next page.

To Any Reader, p. 2

DIRECTIONS Think about the poem. Then answer these questions. Darken the circle by the correct answer.

1. The child in the poem is playing

   Ⓐ on a playground.
   Ⓑ in a garden.
   Ⓒ near the woods.

2. Since the time he was in the garden, the child has

   Ⓐ grown and gone away.
   Ⓑ gone inside the house.
   Ⓒ climbed into the tree.

3. The child is intent on his play. "Intent" probably means

   Ⓐ not paying attention.
   Ⓑ in a tent.
   Ⓒ concentrating.

4. This poem is mostly about

   Ⓐ a boy in a poetry book.
   Ⓑ what happens to little boys.
   Ⓒ how children are alike.

5. The boy cannot be called because

   Ⓐ he is not able to hear.
   Ⓑ the garden is too noisy.
   Ⓒ he is an imaginary child.

6. This poem is called "To Any Reader." But the poet seems to think that

   Ⓐ people will think that the child in the poem is real.
   Ⓑ children will be reading the book.
   Ⓒ his book will never be read.

POETRY PATCH Robert Louis Stevenson wrote many poems for children. Although they were written years ago, we still enjoy them today. You may enjoy poems that are more modern. Have you heard of Shel Silverstein? He is one of the most popular writers of children's poetry today. Find one of his books or some of his poetry on the Internet. Read several of his poems, and write a poem of your own that imitates his style.

Three Wise Women

by Elizabeth T. Corbett

Three wise old women were they, were they,
Who went to walk on a winter day:
One carried a basket to hold some berries,
One carried a ladder to climb for cherries,
The third, and she was the wisest one,
Carried a fan to keep off the sun.
But they went so far, and they went so fast,
They quite forgot their way at last,
So one of the wise women cried in a fright,
"Suppose we should meet a bear tonight!
Suppose he should eat me!" "And me!!" "And me!!"
"What is to be done?" cried all three.

"Dear, dear!" said one. "We'll climb a tree,
There out of the way of the bears we'll be."
But there wasn't a tree for miles around;
They were too frightened to stay on the ground,
So they climbed their ladder up to the top,
And sat there screaming, "We'll drop! We'll drop!"
But the wind was strong as wind could be,
And blew their ladder right out to sea;
So the three wise women were all afloat
In a leaky ladder instead of a boat,
And every time the waves rolled in,
Of course the poor things were wet to the skin.

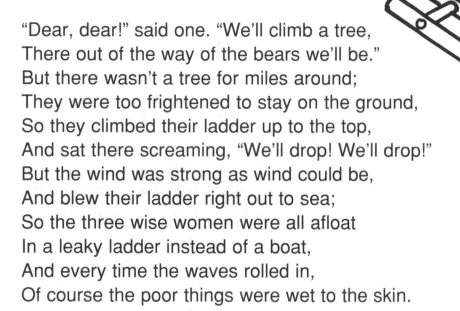

Then they took their basket, the water to bail,
They put up their fan instead of a sail:
But what became of the wise women then,
Whether they ever sailed home again,
Whether they saw any bears, or no,
You must find out, for I don't know.

Go on to the next page.

Three Wise Women, p. 2

DIRECTIONS ➤ **Think about the poem. Then answer these questions. Darken the circle by the correct answer.**

1. What did the most wise woman carry?

- Ⓐ a ladder
- Ⓑ a fan
- Ⓒ a basket

2. What happened second?

- Ⓐ The women went out to sea.
- Ⓑ The women lost their way.
- Ⓒ The women climbed the ladder.

3. To "bail" means

- Ⓐ to remove water from a boat.
- Ⓑ to put up a sail.
- Ⓒ to signal for help.

4. This poem is mostly about

- Ⓐ the proper way to use a ladder.
- Ⓑ how to pick cherries.
- Ⓒ three women getting deeper and deeper into trouble.

5. The ladder would have fallen over because

- Ⓐ it was not a sturdy one.
- Ⓑ it had nothing to support it.
- Ⓒ the women did not know how to climb it.

6. You can tell that

- Ⓐ the women were not wise at all.
- Ⓑ the women made the best decisions they could make.
- Ⓒ the women did not want to pick berries anyway.

POETRY PATCH Using a chair for a ladder, a paper fan, and a basket, act out this poem. Some students may wish to take turns reading the lines of the poem while others do the acting. Assign speaking parts to the actors. Have fun!

Comprehension Activities in Poetry: Grade Four

Answer Key

P. 6: Assessment
1. C
2. B
3. A
4. C
5. C
6. B

P. 8
1. C
2. B
3. B
4. A
5. C
6. B

P. 10
1. C
2. B
3. C
4. B
5. A
6. C

P. 12
1. B
2. B
3. C
4. A
5. B
6. C

P. 14
1. C
2. C
3. B
4. C
5. A
6. B

P. 16
1. B
2. C
3. B
4. C
5. A
6. A

P. 18
1. C
2. A
3. C
4. B
5. C
6. A

P. 20
1. B
2. A
3. B
4. C
5. C
6. B

P. 22
1. B
2. C
3. A
4. B
5. A
6. C

P. 24
1. B
2. A
3. B
4. C
5. A
6. B

P. 26
1. A
2. A
3. C
4. C
5. B
6. C

P. 28
1. A
2. B
3. C
4. A
5. C
6. B

P. 30
1. B
2. C
3. A
4. B
5. C
6. C

P. 32
1. A
2. B
3. A
4. B
5. C
6. B

P. 34
1. C
2. A
3. B
4. C
5. B
6. B

Poetry 4, SV 2048-6

Answer Key (continued)

P. 36
1. C
2. B
3. B
4. C
5. B
6. A

P. 38
1. C
2. B
3. B
4. C
5. A
6. C

P. 40
1. C
2. A
3. C
4. B
5. B
6. A

P. 42
1. C
2. C
3. B
4. A
5. B
6. B

P. 44
1. B
2. A
3. C
4. A
5. C
6. B

P.46
1. B
2. C
3. A
4. C
5. B
6. A